First published in Great Britain in 1980 by
Octopus Books Limited

This edition published in 1985 by
Treasure Press
59 Grosvenor Street
London W1

© 1980 Octopus Books Limited

ISBN 1 85051 087 3

Printed in Hong Kong

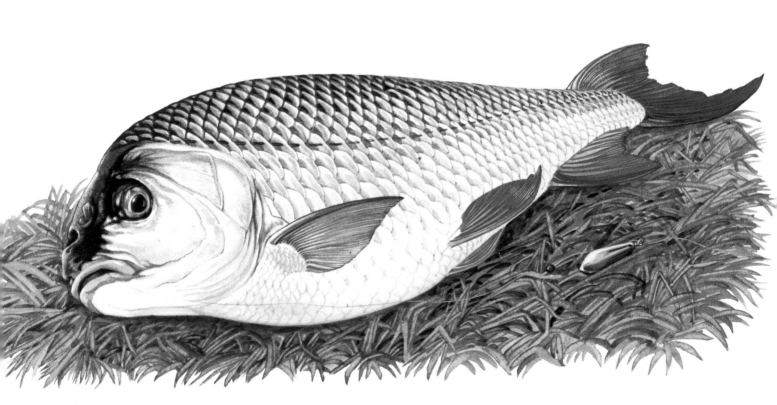

LET'S GO FISHING

MICHAEL PRICHARD
ILLUSTRATED BY KEITH LINSELL

Contents

TREASURE PRESS

A Way of Life

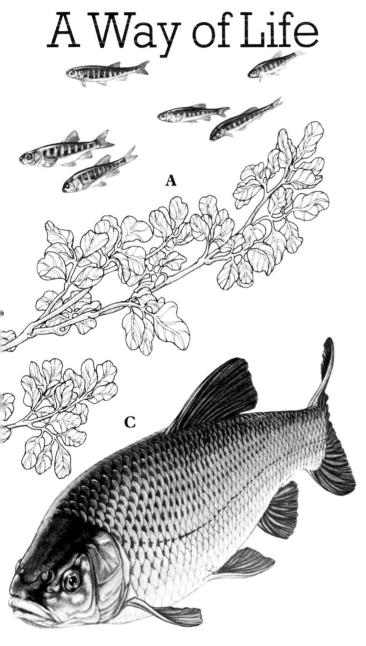

A. Minnows are tiny shoal fish that swim in the clean, cold water that we find at the headwaters of a river.
B. On hot summer days, the rudd will be seen swimming just under the surface searching for insects and larvae.
C. Chub are shy fellows that haunt holes and undercut banks on many rivers and streams. There have been a few introductions of the species into stillwaters, but it is in the river that the chub provides the best sport. D. The small-bodied, crucian carp has no barbules around its mouth.
E. All three varieties of carp have four barbules.

Fish are perfectly adapted to a life in water. They breath by extracting life-giving oxygen from the water. This is done by passing the water across their gills, the fine red-coloured curtains under the gillcase which absorb the oxygen into the fish's body.

Not all fish need the same amounts of oxygen from the water in which they are found. Carp, which can grow to huge sizes need very little. Active in summer when the water is warm, carp burrow deep into the mud during winter to hibernate using little oxygen.

Fish swim and feed at different levels in rivers and ponds. Chub and carp prefer to remain close to the bottom. Both species are bottom feeders but they are also very shy. They dislike the noise that can be created by heavy footfalls on the bankside, and tend to hide among the dark shadows of tree roots.

In midwater you can see those species of fish that can swim easily in stronger water currants. Minnows and bleak feed here where they can escape from larger fish because in clear water the tiny fish have a clear vision of where danger can come from. They are also shoal fish. They crowd together to provide safety in numbers.

Higher up in the water we find the surface feeding fish that are not scared by the bright, light conditions. Probably, the best known of these fish are rudd and trout. Both species will spend hours cruising just under the surface film, waiting for tiny creatures, insects mostly, to fall onto the water within their grasp.

If these fish are disturbed, hearing or seeing you arrive at the bankside, they will sink down slowly into the murky depths or scurry into the safety of the thick weed growth that can be found on the surface of slow-flowing rivers.

If we take a close look at water, through its depth, we find that the deeper the water the less the sunlight can penetrate. Good light, in clean, clear water, makes the water weeds grow. A healthy, lush growth of weed is necessary in any quality fishery because weeds do two things; they provide a continuous supply of oxygen into the water and give a home to the many thousands of tiny animals that are food to all species of freshwater fish.

There is another important role for the water weed. It is to give fish a place to hide.

To become a successful angler, one needs to develop the ability to assess the situation in front of you at the waterside. Before setting up the tackle, look closely at the river or pond. Ask how deep is it, where will the fish be, and why?

The Life of Our Fishes

Pike spawning together in shallow water. Many fish gather together in the annual ritual.

The eggs stick to the leaves of the water weeds where they hatch in the warmth of shallow water. Many of the eggs are eaten by other fish as the parents do not guard the eggs.

The newly-hatched larva has no mouth or gill openings. It attaches itself by a sticky patch on the head to plant stalks for about ten days before it can feed.

Almost fully formed, but not completely pike-shaped, the pike can now feed on minute organisms.

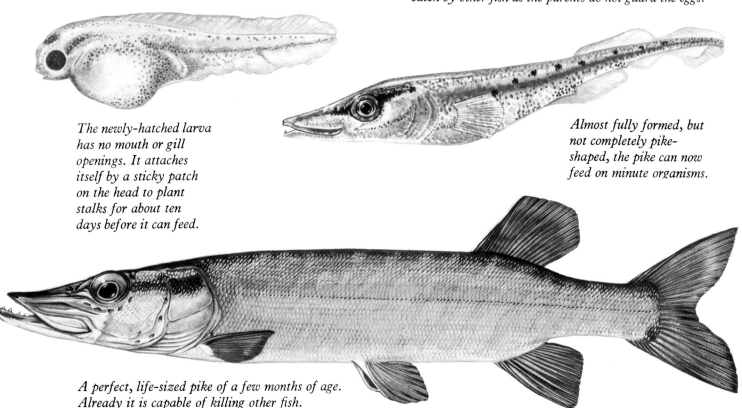

A perfect, life-sized pike of a few months of age. Already it is capable of killing other fish.

Freshwater fish have a similar life cycle to birds. The female fish lay eggs but very few species show any mother-care to the young fish after they hatch. Fish are cold-blooded creatures, so it is left to the water temperature to give the heat that encourages the egg to hatch into the fry, which is the name given to juvenile fish.

Small fish crowd together for protection and to learn all the other behaviour that is necessary for their survival. Very few learn to escape the attentions of larger fish or the many other predators that live alongside water. The pike, possibly the most ferocious fish in freshwater, begins life as an egg that sticks onto weeds. After hatching, the minute pike begin a shoal fish existence. Growing larger, they group themselves together in shoals of fish that are all of the same size . . . then they have no fear of one another! Eventually, a number of large fish will reach huge sizes . . . then the pike becomes the lone killer that we, as fishermen, stalk with rod and line.

If we look closely at the outside of the fish we find that it is encased in a shell of scales. These hard, brittle plates are the fish's skin. They overlap and joint up against each other, keeping out water and disease. On most of our fish, we find a coating of protective slime. It sticks to your hands and landing net but is there

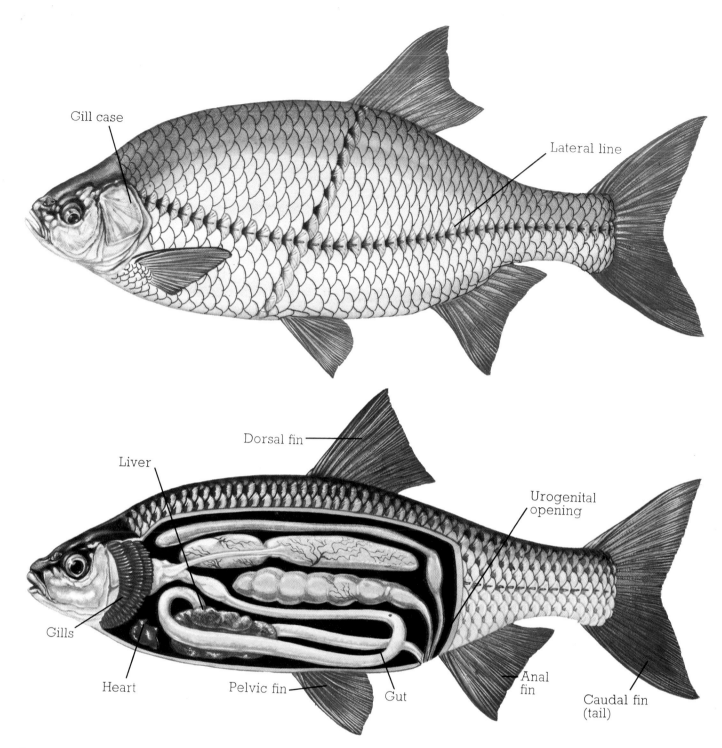

Gill case

Lateral line

Dorsal fin

Liver

Urogenital
opening

Gills

Heart

Pelvic fin

Gut

Anal
fin

Caudal fin
(tail)

for a special reason—to further protect the fish—so handle each fish with great care.

Fish can be identified by the shape of the body, the colour of the fish, the number and position of fins and the number of scales along clearly described lines on the body. Fish grow throughout most of their lives. Unlike animals and birds, they do not have an easily seen child or adult part to their growing up. Fish from healthy waters, where there is plentiful food, will reach bigger sizes, but not necessarily reach maturity, quicker than their less fortunate fellows that strive to grow in a polluted stretch of neglected water.

The feeding style can be readily seen from the position of eyes and mouth on many of our freshwater fish. Generally, those fish that

feed on the bottom of the river or pond have mouths that curve downward or the top jaws may overlap the bottom one. Surface feeders have a longer lower jaw. Fish that grub around for their food, taking any small particle that comes their way, will have no visible teeth . . . they suck the food straight into their mouths.

Predators, fish that live by feeding on other smaller fish, have sharp teeth. The pike is the best example of a creature that is perfectly adapted to catch other fish. His eyes face forward, where they can be focussed on his prey. Shoal fish have eyes placed on the side of their heads. This gives them almost all-round vision, which helps the individual fish to detect a pike in time to warn the members of his family.

9

Nature's Food Chain

We call the cycle of life within the pond, a food chain. The lowliest animals are present in multi-millions and are given a collective name, 'plankton'. These form the food of slightly bigger creatures. The most fertile area is in the bottom mud. Here the larvae of insects and crustaceans feed before undergoing the body change that fits them for an adult life. The bloodworms will eventually become winged midges though some will be gathered by match anglers to use as much sought after hookbait.

Fish fry will eat these tiny creatures, and in turn be eaten by animals higher up on the food chain. Finally, the supreme predatory fish is the pike and, because of his size and ferocity, he has few enemies in the lake, pond or river! But, there are members of the food chain that live outside the fish's territory. On land, we find the otter and the mink, both mammals that live by catching fish! Even a large fish, like the migratory salmon, has to be careful when entering his home river. For at the mouth of the river, where the sea water and freshwater meet, you may see seals. There are two species around our shores; the Atlantic grey and the common seal, both fond of fish!

Small fish are constantly in danger from the air. There are many birds, both waterfowl and

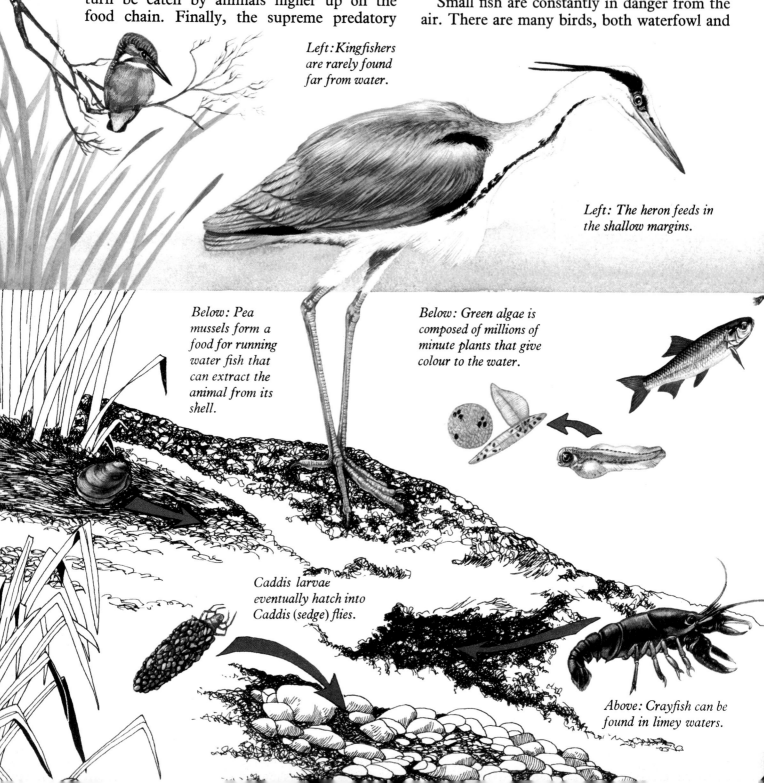

Left: Kingfishers are rarely found far from water.

Left: The heron feeds in the shallow margins.

Below: Pea mussels form a food for running water fish that can extract the animal from its shell.

Below: Green algae is composed of millions of minute plants that give colour to the water.

Caddis larvae eventually hatch into Caddis (sedge) flies.

Above: Crayfish can be found in limey waters.

land birds, that prey on fish. The kingfisher, that flashing, brilliant blue bird of the water-side, is adept at catching tiny fry by diving onto the water's surface to catch little fish that venture too close to the top of the water. In the shallows, the silent grey heron stands, statue-like, waiting for unwary fish to swim within range of his powerful beak. The heron doesn't feed in deepwater, only around the gravel and sandy shallows where he can thrust his beak below the surface skin to find a meal.

The ducks that you see up-ending to feed below the water are known as dabblers, their diet is mainly one of minute larvae, vegetation and algae. The diving ducks, however, along with grebes and terns continuously seek out the shoals of fry . . . they provide a tasty meal.

Now, we arrive at the predator to beat them all . . . man! He has the brain to devise ways of catching fish that are so successful. Man needs to eat, so he catches fish. We anglers are more concerned with the sport of fishing. We must all learn to treat fish with kindness. Catch them, handle them with care as you show your friends the remarkable colour and beauty of the fish and then return your catch safely to the water.

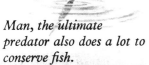

Man, the ultimate predator also does a lot to conserve fish.

Right: Otters are waterside animals that are fast disappearing in Britain.

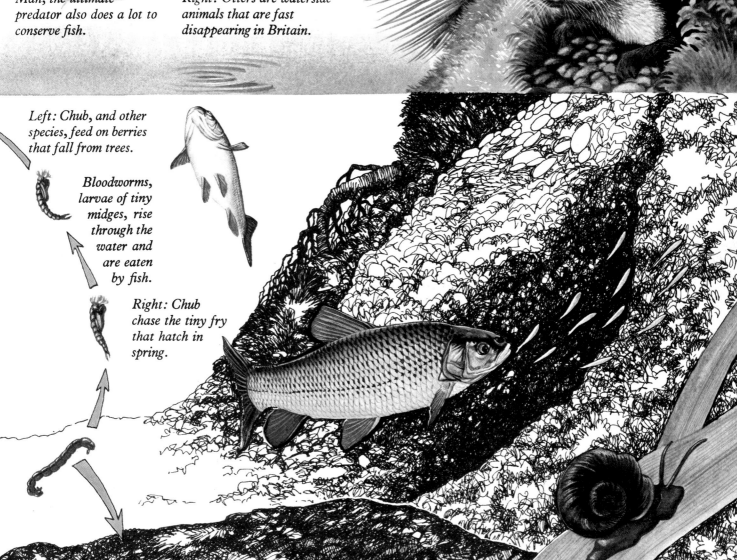

Left: Chub, and other species, feed on berries that fall from trees.

Bloodworms, larvae of tiny midges, rise through the water and are eaten by fish.

Right: Chub chase the tiny fry that hatch in spring.

Fish that Graze

Many times you will hear fishermen describe bream as sheep, a name that tells us something about the feeding pattern of these big fish of stillwaters. They live in shoals that constantly move across the bed of the lake, nosing among the bottom-growing weeds, uprooting roots and disturbing the mud as they search for food.

If you scan the surface of the lake on a calm, summer morning, or perhaps, late into the evening, you may see evidence of bream feeding below. A cloud of small bubbles will burst to the top as the movement of the fish releases a pocket of gas from the debris below.

Sometimes a stream of tiny bubbles will rise between the broad leaves of waterlilies. The colour of the water changes as a fish stirs up the mud around the roots of the plants. A solitary tench is feeding quietly. It doesn't create as much disturbance as the powerful bream shoal.

This indication of feeding tells the fisherman where fish are and the direction in which they are moving. But, the bubbles mean much more! They tell us to put our baits down on the bed of the lake. The bream and the tench expect to find their food among the weeds and mud.

We can lure both species into our fishing pitch by placing food particles where they can find them. This is known as groundbaiting. To catch both bream and tench, we need to halt them as they move from place to place. The groundbait, made from breadcrumbs and other cereals is easily seen by the fish. They stop to feed over the area we have chosen. Now is the time to present a hook bait to them. It is placed in the middle of the groundbaited spot.

Our attractive food will not last long. The fish will soon eat it all. So, from time to time, we throw in pieces of the hookbait as a loose feed that will hold the fish's interest. Eventually, the bream will move on. Each shoal numbers many fish and they all have huge appetites to satisfy . . . so bream fishing sometimes means a long wait before the shoal arrives back from their continual foraging.

There are other shoal fish that graze the vast underwater acres. Roach and rudd follow a similar feeding behaviour, although being smaller in body size they seek smaller amounts of natural feed. Both species can be *pulled* into the swim with a gradual supply of anglers groundbait. The roach, found in rivers as well as stillwaters, always feeds on the bottom. Rudd, which can grow to larger weights, will rise in the water during the warm months of the year. It can often be seen feeding just under the surface on tiny water creatures.

Both tench (left) and common bream graze over bottom-growing weed to find food that is living there and in the mud below. So vigorous are their movements that clouds of muddy water stain the lake, through which burst spirals of tiny bubbles.

Fish that Root

Fish use many senses to find food. They have good eyesight and are able to detect natural food with a smell-taste sense. Their smell organs are specially adapted to life underwater. Some fish, especially the large members of the carp family, have another way in which they find succulent morsels on the bottom. They have barbules, feelers if you like, that sprout from the jaws.

Perhaps the feelers can detect the tiny movement made by a caddis larvae as it drags its house around among the stones? What is important is that all of these fish are bottom feeders that graze. The largest of them is the carp, a fish that can grow to over 40 lb in a lake. There can be some confusion in identifying some carp . . . there are three varieties that vary only in the number and size of scales on their bodies. The common carp is fully scaled. Mirror carp have just a few large scales along the middle line of their bodies, whilst the leather carp has no scales at all. The last two varieties have been *manufactured* by fish farmers by selective breeding. All three types have four feelers, two on the top jaw with one barbule at each corner of the mouth.

The barbel is a fish built for swimming in the strongest currents of big rivers. His body is streamlined and muscular.

Barbel are fish that feed by rooting over stones to find live creatures hiding from them. They have a siphon-like snout that sucks up the gravel, sifting out food from the other material. There are four barbules around the jaws of the barbel which helps us to identify this species.

The gudgeon looks like a miniature barbel with two feelers at the corner of its jaws.

In fast, shallow water, particularly where it races over gravelly bottom, we must look for two other species that feed on the bottom. Grayling, a close relative of the trout, and the flashing, silvery dace are seen darting around searching for food. They work hard, continuously foraging among the stones for the smallest of water creatures that will give the shoals a meal. The shoal moves by unseen command, one moment feeding avidly with heads probing among the stones and then, suddenly, speeding away to the security of deeper water when our carelessly cast shadow crosses the water. To see fish on the shallows we must tread carefully, remembering that the noise made by our footfalls can be felt.

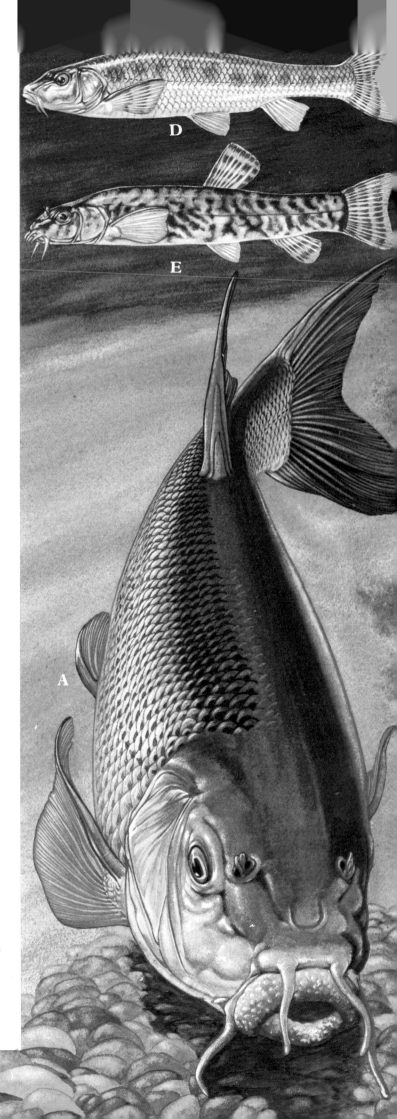

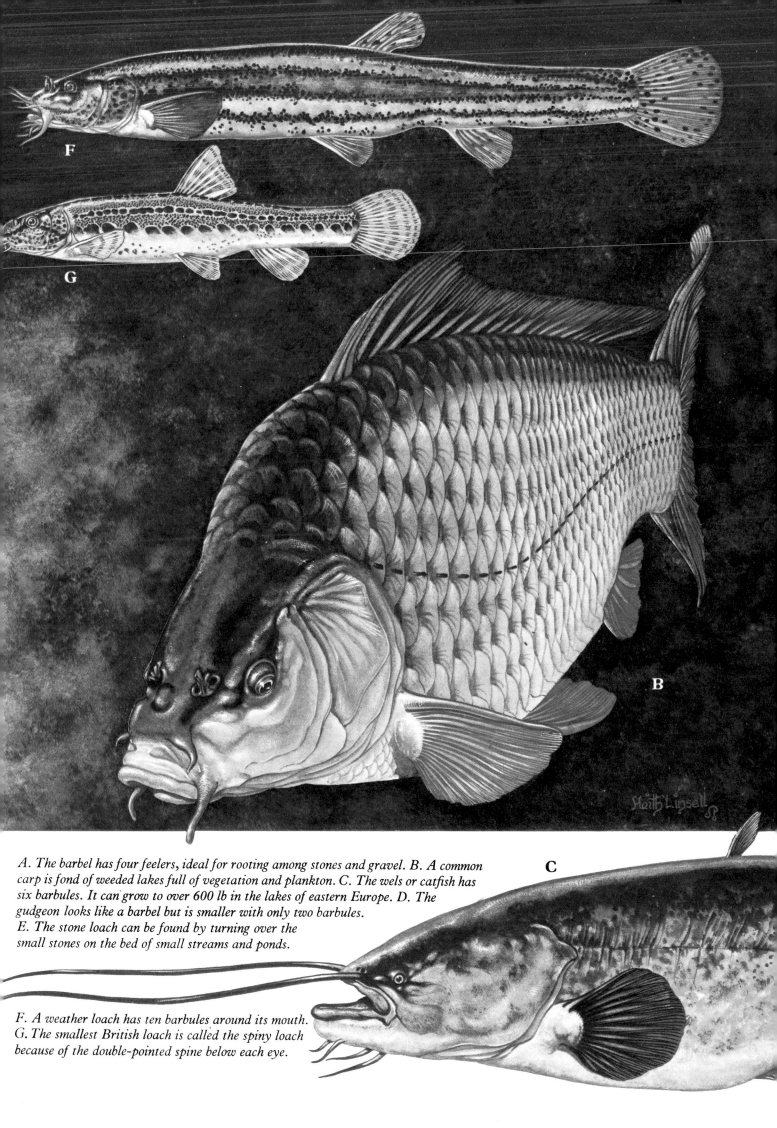

A. The barbel has four feelers, ideal for rooting among stones and gravel. B. A common carp is fond of weeded lakes full of vegetation and plankton. C. The wels or catfish has six barbules. It can grow to over 600 lb in the lakes of eastern Europe. D. The gudgeon looks like a barbel but is smaller with only two barbules.
E. The stone loach can be found by turning over the small stones on the bed of small streams and ponds.

F. A weather loach has ten barbules around its mouth.
G. The smallest British loach is called the spiny loach because of the double-pointed spine below each eye.

Browsing Species

B

A. The ide, or orfe, is a surface fish that can be found throughout Europe. B. Grayling will take flies from the surface, as well as other small food creatures. C. Brown trout, superb fighters, are found in running and stillwaters. D. The ruffe is a tiny, perch-like fish that gives good sport on ultra-light tackle. E. Asp, a sporting European species, is found mainly in rivers. F. The scavenging freshwater eel swims at the bottom of lakes and rivers.

F

Fish that browse are the opportunists of the lakes and rivers. They live by anticipating where food will be and when! In winter, when hard frosts send many types of fish into their form of hibernation, the thick-bodied, suspicious chub will be found feeding.

Chub are solitary fish. They are difficult to see as they favour the holes, undercut banks and other shadowy places of the river or stream. Almost anything will be eaten by this fish; maggots, seeds, fruits, small fish and freshwater crayfish are accepted fare. The smaller chub are thought of as shoal fish, forming a family group as they grow to maturity. When larger they establish a definite territory of their own.

Although a bottom-feeding species, chub change their searching methods for food as the warm months bring new life to the river. They will chase the fry of other fish, but if there is a sure sign of the presence of a big chub it is the fish's habit of lying beneath the overhanging branches of trees that border the river. Here they wait for insects, caterpillers and other morsels to fall onto the water. The feeding chub will rise up, suck in the food and then sink, without any noisy splashing.

Because of this varied appetite, chub can be caught with a variety of baits. They feed at different depths, depending on the season and the water temperature. One place to make your first cast is into the quiet water, where the current swirls around forming an eddy. Chub rarely feed in the strongest currents, they prefer to lie easily, off the main stream.

Eels are the scavengers of freshwater, they clean up dead and dying creatures that sink to the bed of streams and ponds; and so, the eel performs a useful task in freshwater. But they aren't completely freshwater fish at all! All eels begin life in saltwater, far down in the Atlantic Ocean, where they hatch, and begin the long journey to Europe.

There is a fish in our waters that will eat practically anything—indeed, it is almost as fierce as the pike. The brown trout lives in both running and stillwater, will feed on insects that alight on the surface, chase fry of any species, take a coarse fishers bait and slash at an artificial, metal lure. The complete opportunist would be a correct name for this prince of fishes. There is a seagoing cousin called the sea trout that visits freshwater rivers to spawn each year. He differs in colour, adopting a suit of silver scales instead of the brown and yellow of the 'brownie'.

Predators

A predator is a fish that lives by killing other fish. Some of them will feed on other creatures but live fish are their main target. Of course, most fish species will take other, less fortunate, fish at some time or other as nearly every swimming creature displays predatory instincts as they develop from fry to adult fish.

Ask anyone about a fish that stalks others and the pike will be mentioned. Long and sleek, the pike is superbly built for the life it leads, surging out from its favourite ambush lair to smash into an unwary shoal of feeding fish. He

grabs one, then speedily returns to his hiding place. This method of attack can be used by anglers to advantage. We can offer the pike a spinner or wobbling spoon that looks and moves just like a small fish. If we fish it correctly, the pike will tear into the attack and give us the fight of a lifetime!

There are two other predatory fish; the perch, a specialist in the art of camouflage and the zander, which is a species introduced into England from Eastern Europe. We should also mention a fish that one can fish for on the Continent . . . the large-mouth bass. It looks rather like a perch with its spiny first dorsal fin. This fish is not native to Europe, but was

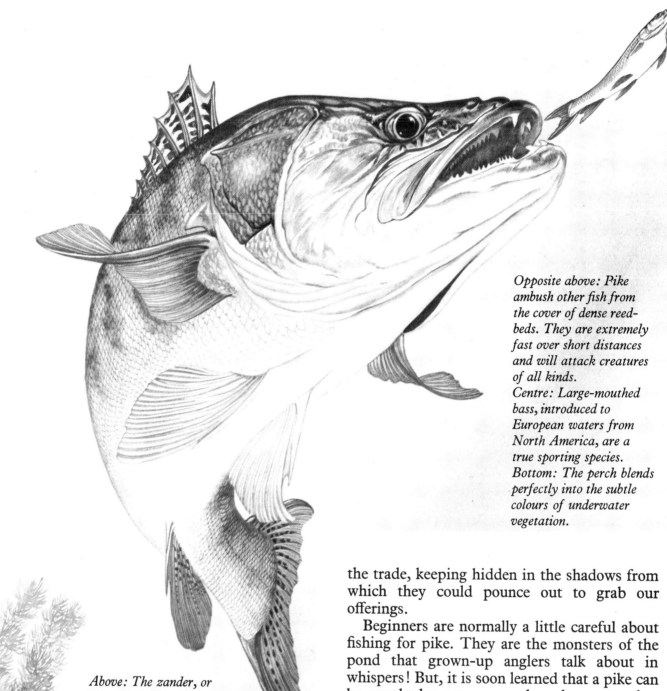

Above: The zander, or pike-perch likes to feed in mid water, chasing small shoal fish.

Opposite above: Pike ambush other fish from the cover of dense reed-beds. They are extremely fast over short distances and will attack creatures of all kinds.
Centre: Large-mouthed bass, introduced to European waters from North America, are a true sporting species.
Bottom: The perch blends perfectly into the subtle colours of underwater vegetation.

brought over from America to increase the number of sporting fish available to anglers. Bass are one of the few species that look after their young. The male guards the eggs in the nest to stop other fish from enjoying a feast. The bass and the perch feed on insects and small water animals when young but as they grow, fish become their daily food.

The favourite fish of most small boys is the one that comes readily to their bait. Most anglers started by catching small perch. They were easy to attract to our worm baits. Anything that wriggled could be lowered on light float tackle alongside a clump of half-hidden tree roots where the little perch were learning the trade, keeping hidden in the shadows from which they could pounce out to grab our offerings.

Beginners are normally a little careful about fishing for pike. They are the monsters of the pond that grown-up anglers talk about in whispers! But, it is soon learned that a pike can be caught by a young angler who approaches the task with care and planning. The small *jack* pike are so speedy that they test your tackle and your ability as an angler to the utmost.

A few years ago the zander, or pike-perch, was brought across from Europe to be placed into waters of the East of England. Within a short time it had established itself as a breeding fish, it thrived and some people say it has become a pest in the slow-running rivers into which it was seeded. It seems that the zander, a sporting fish of speed and power, has been too successful and it seems likely that it will decimate the shoals of bream and roach that have such importance to the match fishermen who travel each weekend to this region to engage in competition fishing. Attempts are being made to prevent the spread of this predator to other rivers of England.

Tackle

Angling in freshwater is a fun occupation. To enjoy the sport one has to have the basic tackle —a rod, a reel, enough nylon line to fill the spool and a few small tackle such as hooks. floats and leads. Simplicity in your approach to the sport, coupled with simplicity in tackle make-up will enable you to learn the craft from the beginning.

Let us look closely at the tackle and how to use it. A coarse fishing rod which can be used in a wide variety of fishing situations, is vital. Choose the best that you can afford. An 11-foot rod will be light in the hand and still have the power to land good chub, tench or even a huge carp. To balance the rod we use a small size fixed-spool reel. Check and make sure that the spool will take about 100 yards of 3-4-lb nylon line. Buy a spare spool, if possible, then load it with 6-lb line to cope with landing larger specimens. Always wind the nylon onto the spool properly. Ask a friend to hold the plastic spool by pushing a pencil through the centre hole. He can apply a little finger pressure, on each side of the spool, to ensure that the line beds down correctly. Running the nylon onto your reel with the maker's spool revolving in this fashion prevents line twist which could make easy casting difficult.

Basically, there are two ways to cast float and tackles; overhead or from a side cast. Which you use depends on where you are fishing. If the bankside is clear of bushes and trees, the overhead cast can be used with most kinds of float. However, there is one type of float that should never be cast overhead—the loaded floats that have weight built into them. They will fly out in front of the split shots causing a mighty tangle. With zoomers, missiles and self-cocking floats it is best to use the sidecast where you are able to swing the tackle out.

Learn to use your fishing reel by practising to cast on your lawn, if you have one, or in some open space. Just tie a small weight to the end of the line, then:

1. Pick up and trap the line on your finger.
2. Swing the rod back, taking a glance to see that there are no obstructions behind.
3. Make the forward casting motion, aiming the rod tip in the direction that you need the tackle to cast to. Release the nylon as the rod tip straightens.
4. After the weight has hit the grass

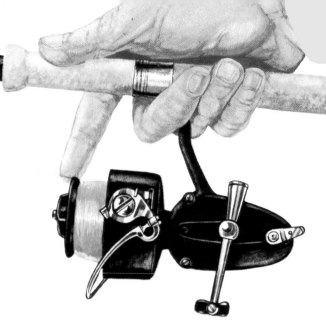

Above: Before making the cast, open the bale arm while trapping the line on your index finger.

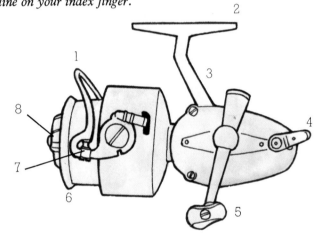

Above: The fixed-spool reel
1. *Bale arm*
2. *Reel seat*
3. *Stem*
4. *Anti-reverse lever*

5. *Handle*
6. *Spool*
7. *Line pick-up roller*
8. *Tension drag nut*

(here we must imagine being at the water-side so allow time for the float tackle to settle) turn the handle of the reel to close the bale arm giving a few extra turns to take up the slack between rod and float.

The ease with which you can cast depends on practise and the amount of lead shot pinched onto the line. This weight will alter according to the float in use.

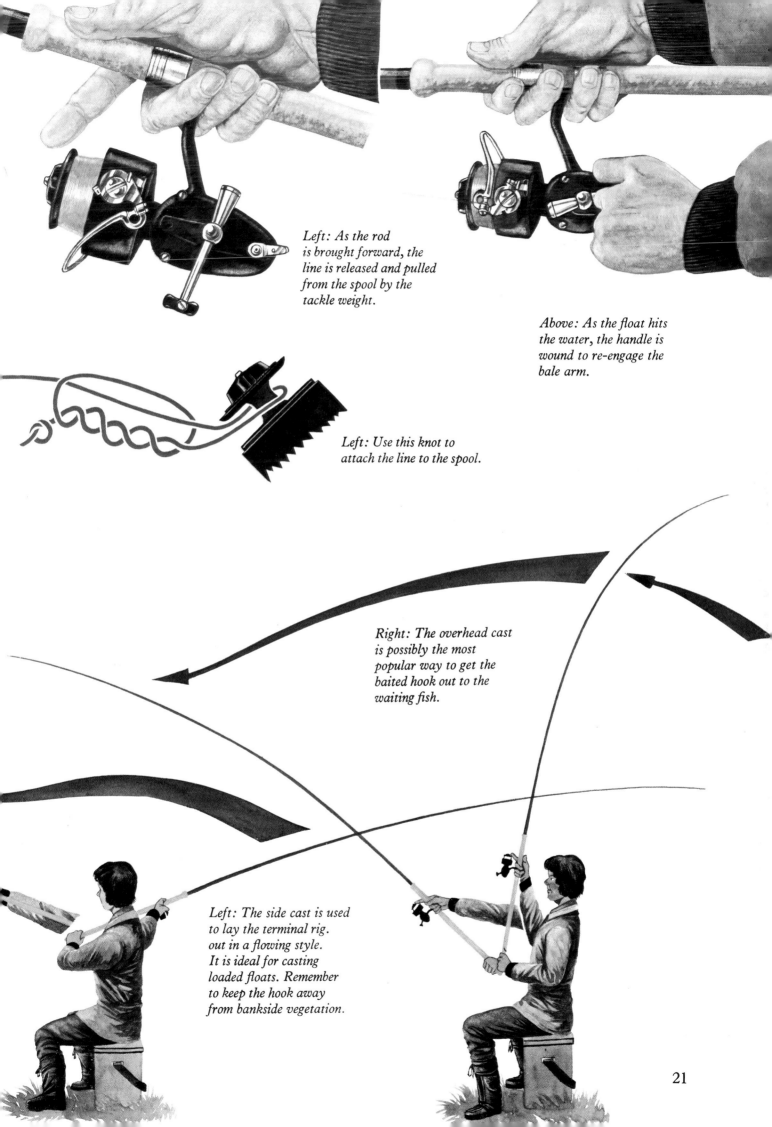

Left: As the rod is brought forward, the line is released and pulled from the spool by the tackle weight.

Above: As the float hits the water, the handle is wound to re-engage the bale arm.

Left: Use this knot to attach the line to the spool.

Right: The overhead cast is possibly the most popular way to get the baited hook out to the waiting fish.

Left: The side cast is used to lay the terminal rig out in a flowing style. It is ideal for casting loaded floats. Remember to keep the hook away from bankside vegetation.

Catching Roach

Roach are by far the most common fish in our streams. These silver-scaled beauties give great sport when the tackle and methods are adapted to the fish's size. We must use a hook size that is correct for the bait. The line, on which the hook is tied, should be the finest that your experience allows you to handle.

So, with your rod, reel and line you can make an approach to the river bank. Before tackling up, you must take a close look at the river. Any reedbeds, patches of underwater weed and the speed of the current will determine how we are to fish. If the river, downstream, is clear of weed and looks to be of even depth you

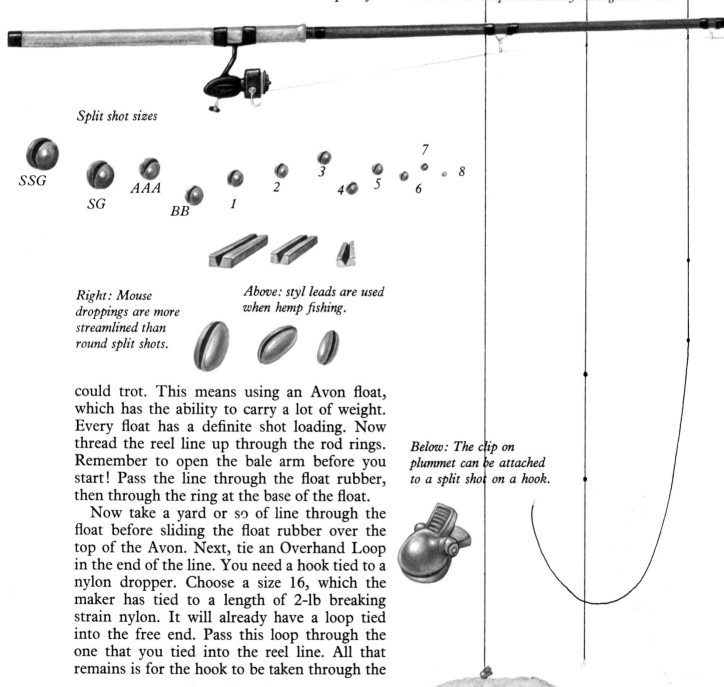

Above left: Plumbing the depth to obtain the correct float setting. Above centre: An Avon float rig set to trot a bait just above the river bed. Split shots are pinched on near to the hook to take the bait down fast to the shoal fish. Above right: A sensitive quill float is used to swim the stream. The shots are placed just below the water so that the bait drops attractively through the water.

Split shot sizes

SSG SG AAA BB 1 2 3 4 5 6 7 8

Right: Mouse droppings are more streamlined than round split shots.

Above: styl leads are used when hemp fishing.

could trot. This means using an Avon float, which has the ability to carry a lot of weight. Every float has a definite shot loading. Now thread the reel line up through the rod rings. Remember to open the bale arm before you start! Pass the line through the float rubber, then through the ring at the base of the float.

Now take a yard or so of line through the float before sliding the float rubber over the top of the Avon. Next, tie an Overhand Loop in the end of the line. You need a hook tied to a nylon dropper. Choose a size 16, which the maker has tied to a length of 2-lb breaking strain nylon. It will already have a loop tied into the free end. Pass this loop through the one that you tied into the reel line. All that remains is for the hook to be taken through the

Below: The clip on plummet can be attached to a split shot on a hook.

small loop and the join has been made.

To present our bait effectively, you need to know the depth of water in the river. Start by attaching a plummet weight to the hook. Now make a swing cast so that the float splashes into the stream at about one rod length out from where you stand. Watch the float closely, if it sinks immediately then the float is set too low. So slide the float higher up the line. If the float lays flat before being pulled under the water by the current, shorten the distance between the hook and float. Make a number of casts until you are certain that the hook is positioned at the riverbed.

Now pinch on the split shot to cock the float and to take the bait down to where the roach

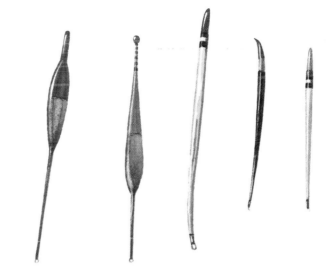

Above: Floats left to right:
Avon
Balsa-bodied antennae

Swan quill
Porcupine quill
Crow quill

Above: A float rod should be long enough to allow easy casting and perfect control when playing a fish. The usual length is between ten and fourteen feet.

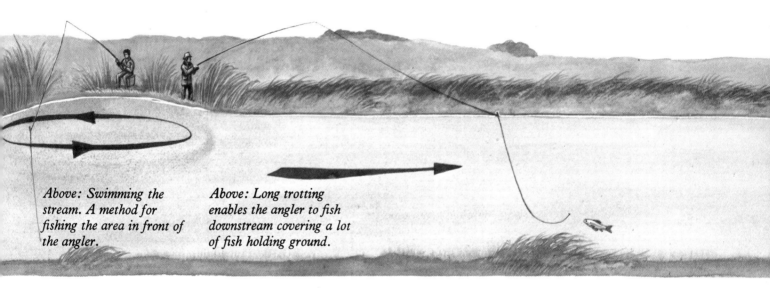

Above: Swimming the stream. A method for fishing the area in front of the angler.

Above: Long trotting enables the angler to fish downstream covering a lot of fish holding ground.

will be feeding. To trot the river, cast the float out to let it be carried downstream at the speed of the current flow. Bites will show as the float dives under the water! In this style of fishing we keep the bale arm open, controlling the run-off of line by gently touching the rim of the spool with the index finger. If we get a bite or when we feel that the float has travelled too far, the bale arm is closed by a smart turn of the reel handle.

Swimming the stream means that the float tackle is cast slightly upstream and allowed to drift down, on the flow, to a point just below the angler. The tackle is then wound in before casting upstream again. The float and shots are lighter, to let the bait flutter down through the water to excite the fish.

Right: When trotting with a fixed-spool reel, control is maintained by applying pressure from the finger to ensure an even flow. The bale arm is left open.

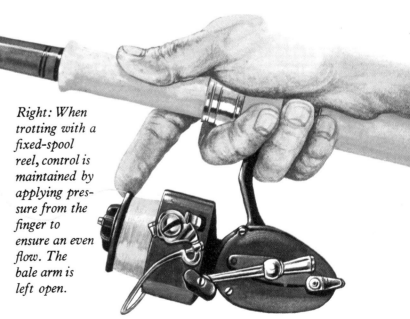

23

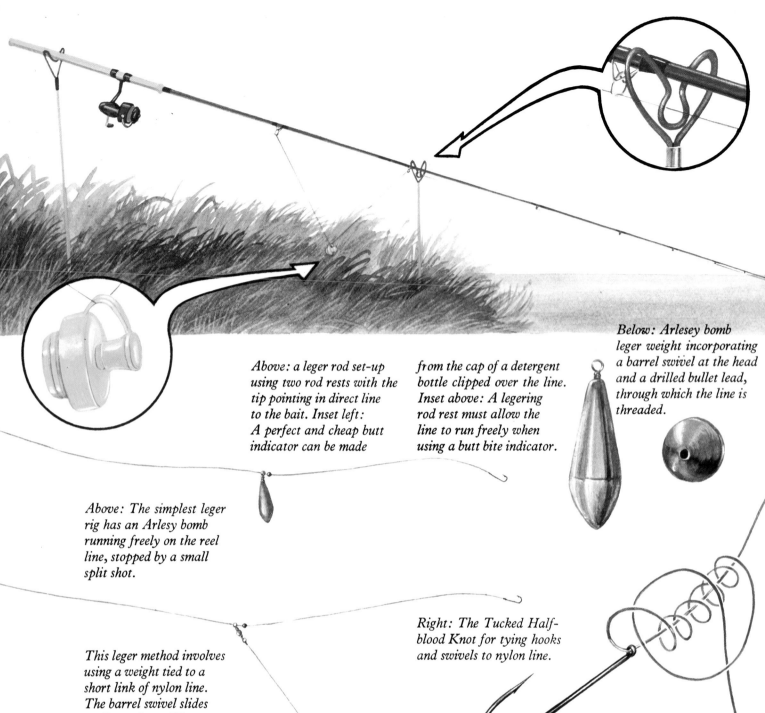

Above: a leger rod set-up using two rod rests with the tip pointing in direct line to the bait. Inset left: A perfect and cheap butt indicator can be made

from the cap of a detergent bottle clipped over the line. Inset above: A legering rod rest must allow the line to run freely when using a butt bite indicator.

Below: Arlesey bomb leger weight incorporating a barrel swivel at the head and a drilled bullet lead, through which the line is threaded.

Above: The simplest leger rig has an Arlesy bomb running freely on the reel line, stopped by a small split shot.

This leger method involves using a weight tied to a short link of nylon line. The barrel swivel slides easily on the reel line.

Right: The Tucked Half-blood Knot for tying hooks and swivels to nylon line.

Legering

Legering is a system where the bait is cast out using only a lead weight to carry the bait to rest on the lake bed. Sometimes conditions, or personal choice, will suggest that it could be a better method than float fishing. Obviously there is no float to show us when a fish takes the bait so we need a simple bite detector. This is called a swingtip. It is a flexible arm that screws into the threaded tip ring found on all good leger rods. The reel line passes out through a ring on the swingtip. When the fish takes the bait, it moves off, pulling the line. This causes the bite indicator to swing up. We strike, by raising the rod tip quickly. This movement

takes in the slack line and sets the hook.

Successful legering relies on having the line drawn tight between the leger weight and the swingtip. After casting out your bait, give the lead time to settle on the bottom. Then, wind in a few turns until the swingtip begins to rise. Now the rig is set to fish effectively.

It is difficult to detect a bite with a rod held in the angler's hand. Therefore we use rod rests. Two of them are necessary for fishing this method and they should be placed about four feet apart. They carry the weight of the rod and keep everything perfectly still. Any movement of the swingtip is then clearly seen. Setting up to fish leger style is important. Position the rod rest so that the handle of the rod lies just below your hand. Then you only

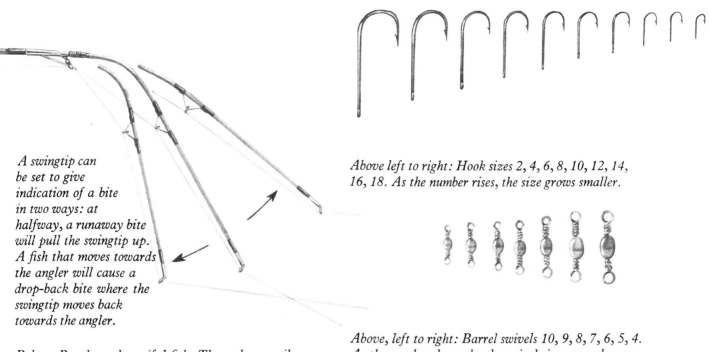

A swingtip can be set to give indication of a bite in two ways: at halfway, a runaway bite will pull the swingtip up. A fish that moves towards the angler will cause a drop-back bite where the swingtip moves back towards the angler.

Above left to right: Hook sizes 2, 4, 6, 8, 10, 12, 14, 16, 18. As the number rises, the size grows smaller.

Above, left to right: Barrel swivels 10, 9, 8, 7, 6, 5, 4. As the number descends, the swivel size grows larger.

Below: Roach are beautiful fish. The scales are silver darkening to a rich, blue-black on the upper body. The fish has bright red fins and the jaws are of equal length.

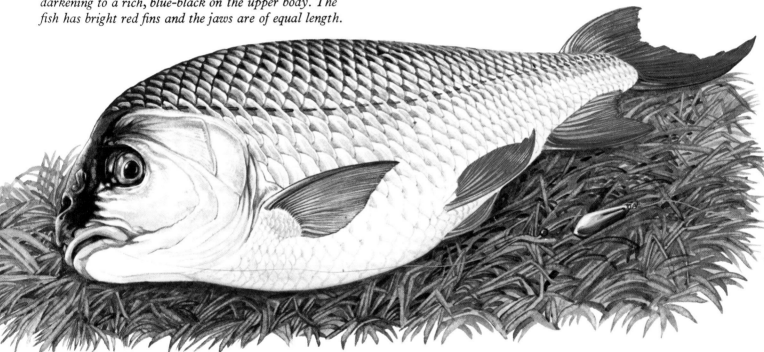

have to move inches to grasp the rod, strike and begin to play the fish.

There are two ways to attach the leger weight to the line. On a clean gravelly bottom, with few obstructions, an Arlesey bomb can be slipped direct onto the line, stopped from moving down to the hook by a No 1 split shot. Or, where there is soft on the bed of the lake, the leger weight can be fixed onto a short piece of nylon that is tied to a swivel that slides on the line. This method allows the weight to sink into the mud but doesn't pull the bait in where fish may not find it.

There is another system that is an adaption of the first idea. It is called the link leger. To make it, a short length of nylon is folded over the reel line and then a number of big split shots are pinched onto the short link. The weights are prevented from slipping by the same No 1 shot. The advantage of this rig is that if the shots get caught up in a snaggy bottom, a sharp pull on the rod will cause the split shots to pull off from the nylon link. So, you do not lose the terminal rig or your fish!

Leger fishing normally catches bigger fish than one would expect when using a float technique. The reel line would be 4-lb breaking strain or thereabouts. Hooks used are of the eyed variety. These are tied direct to the reel line by a Tucked Half-blood Knot.

Legering, which uses a weight to cast the bait, lets you fish at longer distances than float fishing can. The bait can be put on the bottom, no matter what the depth of water is.

Float Fishing for Bream

Bream are a common fish in stillwaters. They can be fished using leger tactics but using a float to catch them is more fun! The shape of a bream's body makes the fish an awkward feeder. It has to stand on its head to suck food into its mouth! Anglers know this, so they adopt a float rig that actually lets them see this.

An antennae float, which has a bulbous balsa wood body into which is fitted a long cane tip, is fixed to the reel line with a float rubber at the bottom only. The split shots are placed near to the hook, with the largest shot three inches from the hookbait. The depth is set so that an inch of flat tip shows above the surface.

As the fish tips up on end to take the bait it gives the first indication of a bite as the float may bob or move sideways. The bream now sinks back to its normal swimming attitude. The bottom lead is lifted (inset) which causes the float to rise and fall flat on the water. A strike made as this happens will hook fish.

Another method used to catch members of the bream family is to Lay On. To do this the line must carry split shot in a graduated pattern. Let us suppose that the float, it could be a small crow quill, is capable of carrying No 1 and No 3 shots. These are spaced so that the two larger shots are just below the mid-water position on the line. These act as bulk shot to settle the float to its correct depth. The small

Bottom: The silver bream is often mis-identified. When mature it looks very much like a small common bream, which is silvery scaled when young.

Below: The zope is a bream found in many rivers and stillwaters on the continent. The dorsal and anal fins are more pointed in this species.

No 3 shot lies on the bottom, about six inches from the hook. After casting and letting the rig settle, the line to the float is drawn tight between float and rod tip. Any movement of the tiny 'telltale' shot, as a bream picks up the bait, will give a positive movement to the float. This method uses a float that is fixed with a rubber at the top of the float with the line passing through the float ring.

Sometimes, when fishing on a lake or pond, a strong breeze will blow the float across the water. This, in turn, continuously moves the bait around on the bottom making bites difficult to see. We can cut down the effect of the wind by using an antennae float, fixed with a rubber at the bottom of the float. After casting the float out, sink the rod tip and wind in some line. This will sink your line below the surface. Now, the breeze has only a slim float tip to push against. The line will not pick up the wind which means that our float will stay where it is cast. You will have to adjust your rod rests so that they point the rod tip down toward's the water's surface. In a strong wind, you can keep the tip just below the waves.

You may have the good fortune to fish a water that is known to contain big bronze bream. If you know they are there, tackle up accordingly. A reel line of 3-4 lb will cope with the powerful fight that can be expected. Tie a No 10 eyed hook direct to the reel line to fish a big bait

A common or bronze bream feeding. The tilted body is characteristic among the slab-sided fishes.
Inset—bottom: The bream lifts the hookbait which raises the shot lying on the bottom.
Inset—left: The float lifts, tilts over and falls flat when using the Lift Float method.

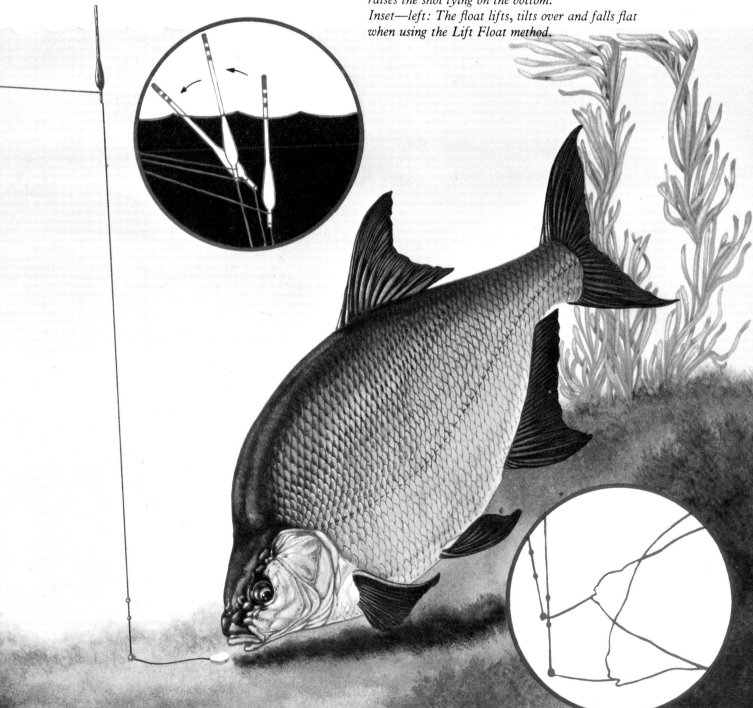

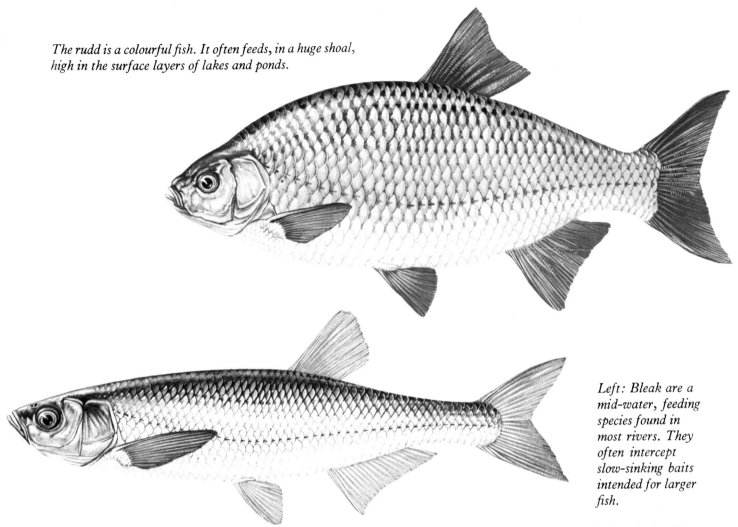

The rudd is a colourful fish. It often feeds, in a huge shoal, high in the surface layers of lakes and ponds.

Left: Bleak are a mid-water, feeding species found in most rivers. They often intercept slow-sinking baits intended for larger fish.

Below: There are two species of stickleback that can be seen in most fishing waters of Europe. The Three Spined

males take on a brilliant red colouring during the breeding season. Ten Spined Sticklebacks are a mottled fawn.

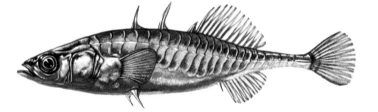

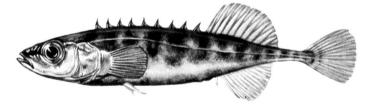

Fishing the Surface Layer

During the warmer months, just after the opening of the coarse fishing season, we often see a golden-scaled fish feeding a little below the surface of lakes and ponds. It is the rudd, a red-eyed, sparkling fish that could be confused with the roach although the rudd has a distinctive longer, lower jaw

Great sport can be expected when we fish a single maggot on a size 18 hook to this fish. With the standard rod and reel, loaded with 3-lb line, we will attempt to lure the rudd on a slow-sinking bait. Fix a self-cocking float by the bottom rubber only to the line leaving a hook length of about two feet. Pinch on a single No 6 shot at six inches from the hook. Before

casting throw a few maggots out onto the water to gain the rudd's interest. Now cast into the area where you threw the loose feed.

The float will cock immediately but the hookbait will only sink down slowly through the depths. A feeding fish, that grabs the maggot, will give a clear indication of its bite on the float. Make certain that the single shot sinks the float to show only about a quarter-half an inch of tip showing. If the float still rides too high in the water, add a further small shot under the float rubber.

There will be days when the rudd are shy in taking your bait. The fish may even sink down to feed on the bottom. Then you will have to employ different tactics. The Overshotted style is a perfect method to overcome both problems. This technique demands that the depth is plumbed accurately. Then the shot load, carried by the float is pinched onto the line. After checking that the float cocks correctly, another split shot is added two inches from the hookbait and the float is moved up by two inches. What happens is that the fish picks up the bait adding the weight of the shot that lies on the bed of the pond to that already strung on the line. This creates too much shot, so the float sinks without the fish having to pull against the buoyancy of it.

This method of shotting a float will work for a variety of other fish species, so don't be too rigid in your choice of fishing techniques. Overshotting works on stillwaters only but the slow-sinking style can be applied to surface feeding fish on slow running streams. You can swim the stream with a slow-sinking bait for bleak and other fish that feed near to the top of the water. A self-cocking float helps to ensure immediate bite detection.

Birds of the countryside provide us with quills from their primary flight feathers. They make super floats. Billy Lane, a master angler from Coventry in England, considers that a crow quill is the most delicate and the most simple to make into a fishing float. All it requires is a whipped-on line ring at the thin end and a float rubber to trap the line at the thick, buoyant end of the quill. There are many other materials used to make floats, each with its own special quality of buoyancy, strength, lightness, price or availability.

On warm, sunny days, rudd will be seen patrolling the surface layers looking for insects that alight on the water. They can be encouraged to feed by throwing out a few maggots that will sink slowly through the depths. Fish a quill float that has been set to cock correctly by wrapping a few turns of soft lead wire around the base (inset). Cast the float tackle out beyond the fish, then draw the float toward the moving fish. The bait will sink with a realistic action.

Over-shotting is a technique that can make all the difference when fishing for shy-biting species. Shot the line carefully so the float cocks perfectly. Then plumb the depth accurately. Add one No. 6 shot to lie on the bottom, When a fish takes the bait, the shot is lifted, adding its weight to the overall shot loading. A fish will feel only the weight of the small shot. The float will sink without any pull from your fish.

29

Fast-running Waters

Barbel, a powerful fish from the streamy water.

Below: Read the water carefully and look in these places for the barbel: over gravel at the head of a deep pool; in the cover of streamer weed; in fast shallow, near to the bankside; among the cover of underwater obstructions.

One fish comes readily to most anglers' minds whenever they stand on the bank of a fast-flowing river—the barbel. A torpedo-shaped, powerful fish that hugs the bottom, rooting among the stones to satisfy a big appetite. The fish is especially fond of places where the speed of the current has gouged out defined channels in the riverbed. For, it is into these gullies that the natural food will be swept. It follows that we must fish our baits right into the heart of the barbel's domain if there is to be any chance of hooking one.

Fishing this kind of fast water is best done with a leger rod, 6-lb nylon and a lead weight that will hold in the flow. So, choose a coffin lead to hold the bait where the barbel can find it. This lead has sharp corners that will dig into the bottom, rarely rolling out from the fastest flow. The hook, a No 6, is tied direct to the reel line which needs to be at least 6-lb breaking strain, for you have to fight both a strong fish *and* a powerful current.

Fishing above average flows will mean that we use no bite indicator other than the tip of the leger rod. Barbel, fished for where the current speeds through, are not shy biters . . . they grab the bait quickly and positively and they probably think that it will be swept away from them downstream!

There are small rivers where barbel can be fished for in conditions of gentle flow. The fish do not have such sharply defined feeding places, they spread throughout the river browsing among the trailing weed that grows in these soft-flowing streams. Here the barbel fisher changes tactics from a static bait to one that is given life by the leger weight. This method uses a drilled bullet weight that rolls across the current searching out places where barbel might be lying.

The bait is cast across the river into a stretch of clear channel between the weed fronds. The lead then rolls over the clean bottom to fetch up against the outer edge of the weeds. It is here that barbel might well chose to hide, awaiting food that is brought downstream. The rod tip remains as the bite detector, the biting fish pulls the tip around sharply, but, in water with very little current we may have to use a bite indicator on the tip. Called a

quivertip, it is really a sensitive extension of the tip section that will be easily jerked round by a feeding fish that takes the bait. Barbel seem to hunt using the feelers around their jaws. They also appear to be able to smell meat baits. So, anglers have offered them cubes of luncheon meat and sausage on their hooks.

Dace, a small silver fish, is another species associated with fast-running water, although dace prefers the shallows. This area of the stream is not easy to fish because of the tumbling water that throws a float around making a bite difficult to see. One way to combat the current is to fish a short hook length below a grayling, self-cocking float trotted downstream.

Below: Southern Barbel are found in Spain, Italy and France.

Right: Dace are small, silver fish that like the highly oxygenated conditions found in the shallows and rapids of rivers and streams.

Slow Waters

The gentle flow of a big river, the almost still-water of a canal or the tiny, meandering stream of the flatlands can be a joy to fish. In these waters, nearly all of our fish species can be found. When rivers have a quiet even flow, fish are more spreadout. The habitat offers many more places that are suitable for breeding and feeding. In fact, the slow-flowing river tends to have larger specimens swimming in it. This is because the fish do not expend so much energy finding their daily food needs so they convert the available food to make body weight.

We can fish either of our two methods. It is nice to float fish. There is an element of control, learned by hours spent on the riverbank, that a fisher can exercise over the tackle. By varying the choice of float every inch of the river can be searched for feeding fish. An Avon float will carry the bait downstream to fish that may have been scared by footfalls, as you arrived at the waterside. The balsa/cane stick float will ride perfectly down through streamy water that is less turbulent than one would use the Avon to fish. Stick floats are a must in the box of the angler who uses casters as hookbait.

In the slack water, found where the river cuts back into bays, the delicate quill floats

A. Moderlieschen or Belica are fish of the dace group, found in fisheries of central Europe. B. Stromer or Soufie look like chub that have a broad purple stripe from eye to tail fin. C. Schneider, a bream-like

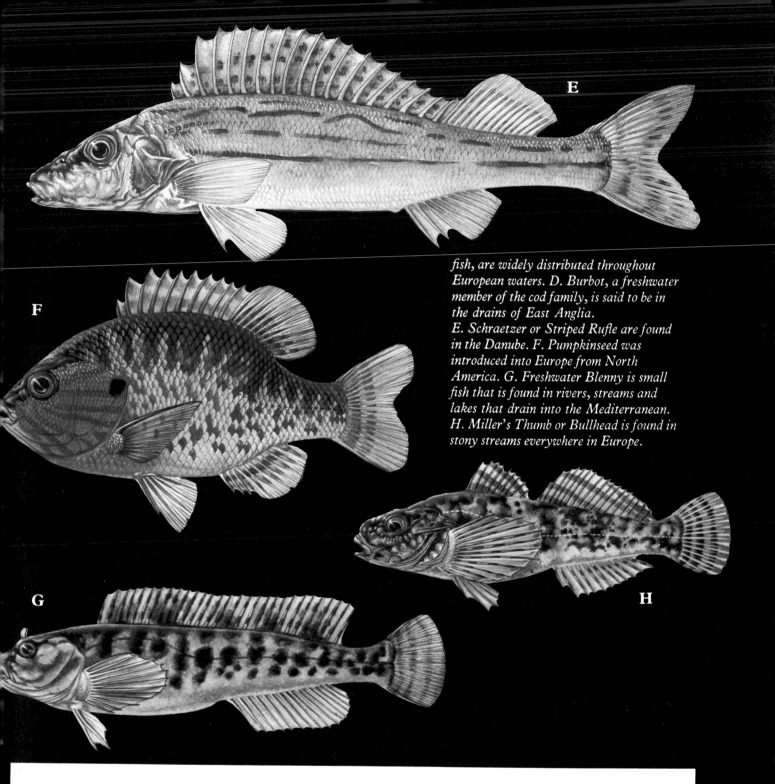

fish, are widely distributed throughout European waters. D. Burbot, a freshwater member of the cod family, is said to be in the drains of East Anglia.
E. Schraetzer or Striped Rufle are found in the Danube. F. Pumpkinseed was introduced into Europe from North America. G. Freshwater Blenny is small fish that is found in rivers, streams and lakes that drain into the Mediterranean. H. Miller's Thumb or Bullhead is found in stony streams everywhere in Europe.

reign supreme. They can be so lightly shotted for the shy-biting fish that live here.

The river may be wide, yet still fishable with a float. We need a float that has enough weight to be able to cast well out across the water. There are many with fancy names. But, a loaded float is a necessity when trying to fish under the opposite bank. Your approach to fishing the distant areas with a zoomer is subtle. There is no need for heavy split shot to get the float across the river, it has a metal weight inside the body of the float, so the line can be very lightly shotted down to the hook.

Of course you can leger this river. Only use the smallest of weights to hold the bait on the bottom. Fish that live in slack water have time to inspect the bait, strong currents are absent so the fish has all the time in the world to decide whether it wants to gobble up your bait. If a fish feels resistance, caused by a heavy weight, it will drop the bait. A feeding fish needs to be able to take a bait in its mouth, then move a short distance to give you a clear indication on the swingtip or butt bobbin that you have a bite.

Don't always float fish or leger at distance. Often fish are lurking under the bank downstream from your fishing pitch. A lot of food drops into the water from the vegetation that grows and hangs over the water. An occasional cast to fish this water will often bring a surprise.

Small Streams

Each of our many rivers is fed by a multitude of small feeder streams that add water, at intervals, as the river flows to the sea. Often we will find a stream that seems hardly wide enough to contain fish. Walk the bank for a short distance and you will see that the stream is not even in width nor is the depth at all even. At the widest places, the stream will become shallow with just a few inches of water creating gravelly runs.

As the stream narrows the amount of water pushes faster, through the gap between the banks like a miniature rapid. This water pressure often gouges out a deep hole below the narrows. As the fast stream turns in a curve, seeking a lower level, the current undercuts the bank. There will be branches from trees brought down by winter gales that lie half immersed in the flow.

Each of these holes, deeps, shallows and natural obstacles create a habitat for fish to live in or among. The changing depths suit different species of fish; some are better equipped to cope with the violent water pressures of the fast runs while the slow-moving fish would use the quiet backwaters.

There is little space to use a long rod. A

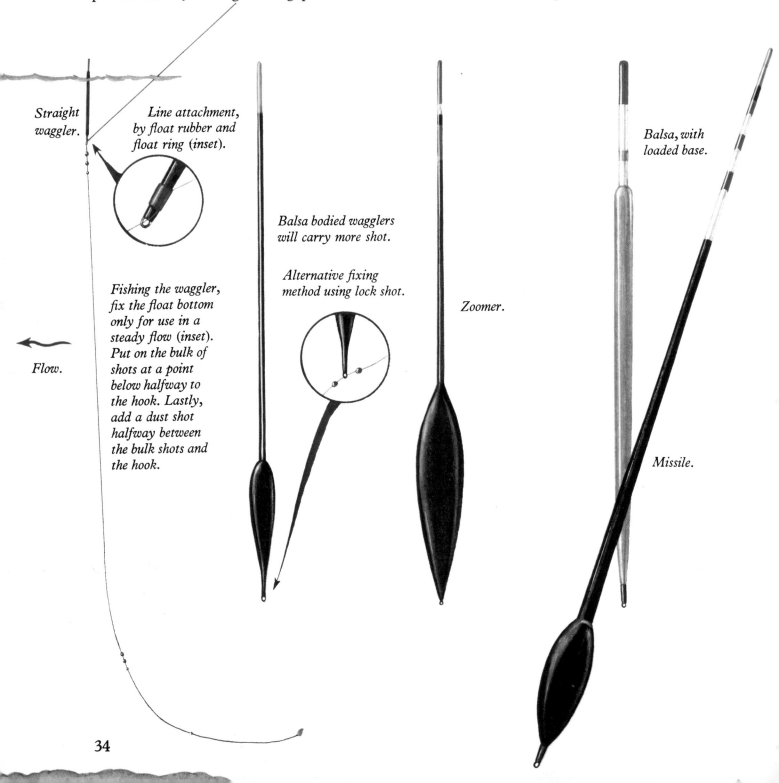

Straight waggler.

Line attachment, by float rubber and float ring (inset).

Balsa bodied wagglers will carry more shot.

Alternative fixing method using lock shot.

Fishing the waggler, fix the float bottom only for use in a steady flow (inset). Put on the bulk of shots at a point below halfway to the hook. Lastly, add a dust shot halfway between the bulk shots and the hook.

Flow.

Zoomer.

Balsa, with loaded base.

Missile.

34

Above: A bait can be free-lined in streamy water. The current will carry a bait to shy fish. Sometimes you only

need the smallest of split shot (above right), pinched on to the line, to enable you to cast a light bait.

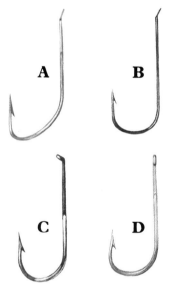

Left: Four hooks for the freshwater angler:
A: Spade-end, 'Crystal', gold forged—for maggots and casters;
B: Spade-end, blued, extra-fine wire—for single maggot bait;
C: Round bend, turned-down eyed hook—for legered baits.
D: Round bend, straight-eyed, gold forged—for carp fishing.

Right: Try legering in those hard to get places by using the fingertip, touch legering method but watch out for the rod-wrenching bite from a big specimen !

shorter spinning rod is best when there are overhanging branches or thick bankside vege-tation. Light in the hand, this style of rod can be poked through gaps between the bushes. It is rare to find a small stream that can be fished with trotted float rigs. There is so much change in depth that an ultra-light leger rig or free-lined bait will offer the better chances.

To leger the holes in the stream, start by tying an eyed hook direct to the reel line. Pinch on a single AAA split shot at about a foot from the hook. Cast the bait into likely places, holding the rod in one hand and the line between your finger and thumb. Tiny, plucking bites will be felt as a tremor on the line. The lead will tend to move around in any current but experience will show the difference between the two movements. Bites from a larger fish will produce a sharp movement that will pull the rod tip over. I find that a small lobworm is a superb bait on the small stream. The rain

washes worms from the surrounding fields into the land drains and into the streams.

Where the depth of water is really shallow you might try your hand at free-lining. This is the simplest of angling methods. Just a hook and its bait. The cast is made using the weight of the worm or ball of paste. Swing the bait out, through a gap, then let it drift down on the current. Keep the bale arm, on the reel, open and adjust the speed of line running off the spool by applying a light pressure on the rim of the spool. A stiff forefinger will become extremely sensitive to the pull of current or a bite from a fish. Strike before closing the bale arm, then flip the handle around.

Above: The pike is a superbly camouflaged fish. It hides in thick weed beds, ready to pounce on unwary shoal fish.
Below: An eight-feet long hollow glass fibre spinning rod is made in two equal sections. Spinning lures are connected to the reel line, with a wire spinning trace. At least two barrel swivels are incorporated within its length.

Pike Fishing

Pike fishing is something that gets into the mind of anglers as autumn approaches. With summer gone, the weeds die back and the first frosts put a sparkle onto the waterside trees. It is a time for keeping warm by moving. Admirable weather just suited to spinning for the toothy monster'.

Spinning is an art. The presentation of a piece of metal, into which the maker has built a tantalizing action, that this fish will attack. Sometimes the lure looks fishlike, others do not resemble anything that swims. The success of a spinfisherman is in how he uses the artificial lure.

By varying the speed of retrieve, the bait can be made to swim at different depths. Or, the bait can be wound back in a *stop-start* fashion. This will make the lure behave as though it was a wounded or frightened fish. When the lure acts in an interesting way then the pike begins to show his interest. From one position, on the bank, you can cover a lot of water with your spinner. Make a cast to the left, then to the right and finally a cast straight out in front of you. The pike is a crafty fish. He may have seen the spinner travelling through the water on the first cast and his mind says, that is something to eat but cautions him to take a better look. So, he may move out into the stream to intercept the lures as it travels past on another cast. If he takes, you will feel the lure go solid in the water. The rod will arc over, and the fun begins. Your drag setting, on the reel, has already been set so the fish cannot break the line with wild lunges or a fast retreat into its lair.

Pike have to be played carefully. They are strong and know the river or lake better than you do so every sunken tree is a hazard around which the pike can drag your line. Try to keep up a steady pressure on the fish. If he runs out into open water, let him go. There is no danger of losing a fish that fights in the open!

Bring your fish quietly to the net when it shows a definite sign of being beaten. Avoid a theatrical show by yourself or those bankside admirers that will crowd around when the pike comes to the net. Slip the net into the water, lift the rod tip to bring the pike over the rim of the net and lift. Then the fish is yours. So, that was exciting but now we need to get the fish unhooked. Start by inserting the gag,

carefully, between the fish's jaws. When you are certain that it has held, take your pliers and grip the shank of the treble hook. Twist gently and push down to release the barb.

So, we have time to admire the fish. Pike are beautifully-shaped fish that can give a fantastic fight. They deserve to be put back into the water with care, for that one pike may well grow to be a monster that you might hook again in ten years time!

You will find that spinning hooks the small and medium sized fish. The older, bigger pike do not want to chase spinners. They would rather pick up a deadbait from the bottom, expending little energy for the meal.

Below: A deadbait can be cast out to lie on the bed of a river or pond. The hook is attached to a short link of wire trace.

Set up your rod on two rests with the tip pointing in a direct line towards the bait. A bobbin, on the line, between the reel and the first ring will give an immediate indication of a bite.

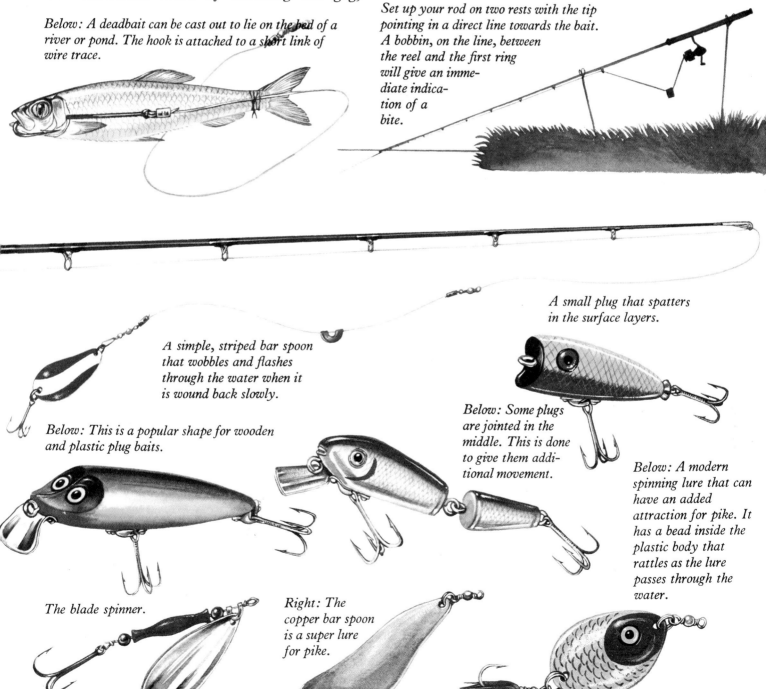

A simple, striped bar spoon that wobbles and flashes through the water when it is wound back slowly.

A small plug that spatters in the surface layers.

Below: This is a popular shape for wooden and plastic plug baits.

Below: Some plugs are jointed in the middle. This is done to give them additional movement.

Below: A modern spinning lure that can have an added attraction for pike. It has a bead inside the plastic body that rattles as the lure passes through the water.

The blade spinner.

Right: The copper bar spoon is a super lure for pike.

The Angler's Hookbaits

Anglers talk of using this or that bait. What they are doing is to present, on a hook, something that the fish will accept as natural food. Sometimes the hookbait is a food that the fish could expect to find drifting down the river or sinking through the depths of a lake. Seeds, fruits and worms also have their place as baits.

We have brought a man-made bait to fishing. The loaf of bread must be the most successful lure for fish that man has ever devised. It white, but it could be bought coloured red, yellow or bronze! The man that breeds them adds colour feed to make them more attractive to fish.

Worms are a bait for big fish. They can be bought from a tackle shop, although I prefer to gather my own. They come from the lawn after a shower of rain has fallen. As darkness comes, the worms move up to the surface where they crawl among the grass eating the rotting grass.

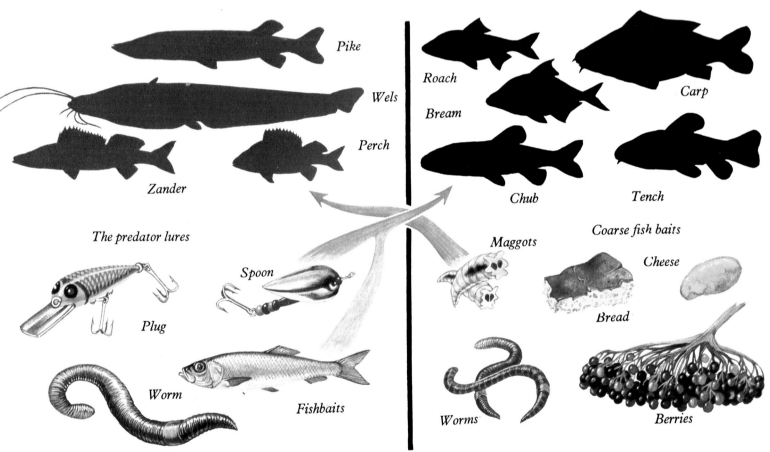

Pike

Wels

Perch

Zander

Roach

Bream

Carp

Chub

Tench

The predator lures

Plug

Spoon

Worm

Fishbaits

Maggots

Coarse fish baits

Cheese

Bread

Worms

Berries

provides paste, flake, crust and when stale a loaf can be dried, then ground, to make groundbait. What more could we ask? Bread is made from wheat. There are other cereals that we can use as hookbait. The maize that chickens eat (we call it sweetcorn) has recently come to the front as a hook bait. Packaged neatly in a tin, it is a bait that can be used on a fishing trip then placed in the refrigerator to keep for the following outing.

Maggots are the popular bait for anglers of all ages. We get them by keeping huge colonies of flies breeding at maggot farms. There are several kinds of maggot, though we only need to buy the popular variety. Sometimes it is

Any sudden vibration and the worms slither back into the packed earth. Catch the worms by grasping them firmly between thumb and forefinger. You may have to pull them, gently, out from among the mass of holes that they bore. Keep the worms in a sealed tin, with air holes punched into the lid. Add some grass or moss.

In the height of summer, a lot of creatures fall from overhanging trees into the water. Caterpillars, grubs, butterflies and spent insects are all food for the waiting fish. Trout, grayling, chub and dace all take insects from the surface of the streamy water, lying in wait they face upstream to snatch the titbits that are washed down to them.

Weather

Fish are like any other living creature, in that they react in a number of different ways to the weather. The heat, of the water in which they live, and the amount of oxygen available to the fish are the two most important factors we have to consider when we try to find fish.

Fish can rise or sink into the deep water according the temperature that they find most comfortable. They can also seek life-giving oxygen by moving closer to places that cause oxygen to be taken into the water, such as waterfalls, canal locks that spurt water through

How weather affects a stillwater. On a hot day in summer—fish are at or near the surface. On a cold winter's day—fish are on or near to the lake bed.

arrive. They fall into a state of partial hibernation. Occasional sunny days, in early spring, may bring them out to feed but both species cannot be fished until mid-June.

In summertime, we find a complete reversal of water temperature. The warmest water is just under the surface of the lake. As the depth becomes greater, so the water gets a lot colder. Fish that use little oxygen can rise to feed near the top of the water, for warm water contains less oxygen than the colder water.

Wind on the water also plays a part in our choice of where to fish. A lot of natural fish food is brought to the creatures by breezes that blow off the land mass. Tiny insects and

On a windy day, with moderate temperatures, fish will feed in well-oxygenated water and will follow food that is driven onto the downwind shore.

the control gates, fast-running streams and streams that run into a lake.

Rainfall and wind sweeping across a lake also bring oxygen into the water making the living conditions better for the inhabitants. Some fish, like carp and tench do not need the same quatities of oxygen as trout or barbel, so they are found in deep lakes often surrounded by trees. The trees drop an enormous amount of leaves into the lake every winter. These decay, releasing dangerous gas.

In winter, we find that the warmest water is at the bottom of lakes and ponds. Fish tend to feed right on the bottom. Carp and tench stop feeding altogether, as the cold months

seeds fall onto the water and generally they are swept across the lake to the windy side. It may be slightly uncomfortable, but there is a proven case for fishing into the wind. Also, as the wind crosses the surface it cools the upper layers of water. This makes the water sink down to be replaced by warmer water that is drawn up to the top of the lake. This constant movement of water mass brings a lot of small animals up from the deeper parts of the lake where they become food for surface fish.

Rivers are much less affected by hot weather. They are fed by water that seeps through the ground. It keeps on the move, so doesn't absorb heat as a stillwater does.

Fishing in Summer

Left: Carp will rise up to take food from the surface of the water. A floating crust makes an attractive bait presented on the simplest of angling rigs.

Above and below: Another simple rig, the lift float using a small piece of peacock quill, can be used to catch summer tench.

As the sun begins to gain warmth in early spring, the freshwater fisherman begins to take an active interest in the rivers and lakes. For three months his tackle has been gathering dust in the boxroom or under the stairs. The fish have had a holiday, a time to breed and begin their major feeding season. Winter rains have flushed out the gathered debris from the rivers leaving the water sweet and alive.

You may choose to open the new fishing year by finding a tench pond, where these large yellow-green fish are grubbing around the roots of the newly-emerged water plants, sending up strings of minute bubbles as they search for bloodworm. Mighty splashes will tell us that there is an even bigger fish at work out in the open water, around the lilypads. The carp are feeding on the surface insects.

You can observe this feeding behaviour and put it to good angling use. If the carp will take his food from the top of the water, give him a bait floating on the lake. With your float rod and the heavier line (6 lb nylon will hold a big fish in open water) try to catch a carp. Tie a No 8 eyed hook direct to the reel line. Now you need a crust torn from the side of a fresh loaf. Insert the hook into the crust, hiding as much of the metal as you can. Carp can be very crafty! They are often called *hook shy* by anglers that specialize in stalking them. Dip

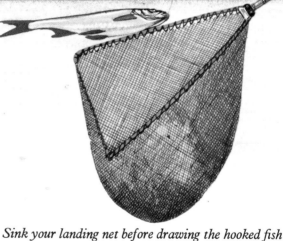

Fish need room to move around within the keepnet. Overcrowding removes scales and slime from the fish's body.

the crust into the water for a fraction of a second. It will absorb enough weight for you to make a good cast. Try to land the crust alongside the patches of weed that are sprouting up. Put the rod into its rod rests and leave the bale arm open.

You can clip on a leger bobbin, or fold a piece of silver paper over a loop of line between the first and second rod ring. This acts as a bite indicator although I prefer to watch the crust. A feeding carp makes a lot of noise when it takes a surface bait. If the crust disappears let the line run from the spool. Keep watching the line closely. As soon as it stops peeling off, close the bale arm and wind slowly. When you

feel the line go tight, strike hard. Then the fight starts in earnest.

When you feel a slowing down of the fish's movements you must apply more pressure into the playing of the carp. Never let the fish have any slack line at all . . . any sudden movement by your hooked fish will cause a broken line! Landing a carp or any other big fish must be done with care. Use a landing net that is big enough for the size of fish that you expect to catch. Ensure that the carp is ready to be netted. Don't make wild jabs at the carp with the rim of the net. Take your time and draw the fish in one positive action over and into the net. It is not a good thing to put large fish, such as carp, into a keepnet. But, if you must do it please see that the net is a large one with soft, knitted, netting that will not damage the fish's scales and fins.

Sink your landing net before drawing the hooked fish across the rim. Then lift the net cleanly from the water.

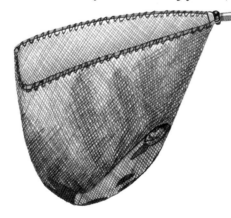

Right: The mesh of a modern, knitted, nylon net is soft and knotless causing fish no harm in landing or keeping them.

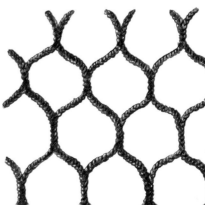

Fishing in Winter

Left: A warm angler is an efficient fisher. These clothes will keep you warm and dry on the wildest of winter days. A wool bobble hat; two jumpers are better than one; quilted, waterproof parka with hood; mittens that leave fingers free to tie knots; thick trousers with, perhaps, pyjama trousers underneath; insulated, waterproof boots.

As the first frosts come stillwaters begin to prove harder to fish, so many anglers turn to the rivers and streams. Fish are far more active —after all, they have to keep swimming to hold position in the flow. Being active throughout the year, the fish's food requirement never ceases, although it may slow up.

It is cold so anglers wrap themselves up in warm clothing. The fish make for the slight warmth that is present in the deep runs. They will not dash after a float fished bait so we resort to legering a static bait—one that is

Left: The float to bait depth is fixed by a single float rubber fitting snugly above the balsa body of this wire-stemmed, self-cocking float.

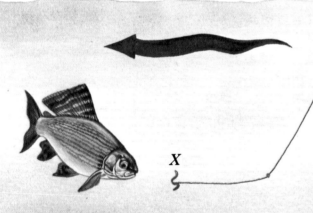

Trotting for grayling in a fast stream. Holding back the float, by slight finger pressure on the rim of the spool, will keep the bait trotting ahead of the float X. A bait that drags along behind the float Y will not show a clearly indicated bite.

X   Y

fished hard on the bed of the stream. Don't throw in a lot of groundbait, the fish will not be attracted by large lumps of feed. Better to feed the swim a little and often when fish show.

Try a small amount of feed legered from a swimfeeder. This is an open-ended container when using cereal feed, or, it could be a block-end feeder if you are fishing with maggots and want to have a few dribbling downstream from the baited hook. The advantage in casting the groundbait out instead of throwing it to the fish is that you can be far more accurate when using a swimfeeder. You know that the feed will lie in close proximity to the terminal tackle.

If you live near to the East Anglian fens in England you are near to the home of the zander. This is a fish that grows large and will

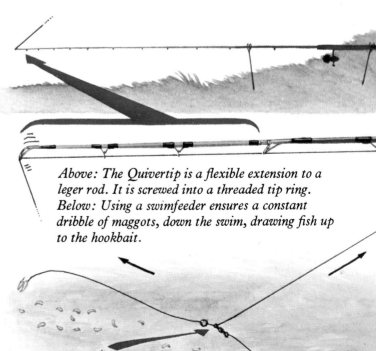

Above: The Quivertip is a flexible extension to a leger rod. It is screwed into a threaded tip ring. Below: Using a swimfeeder ensures a constant dribble of maggots, down the swim, drawing fish up to the hookbait.

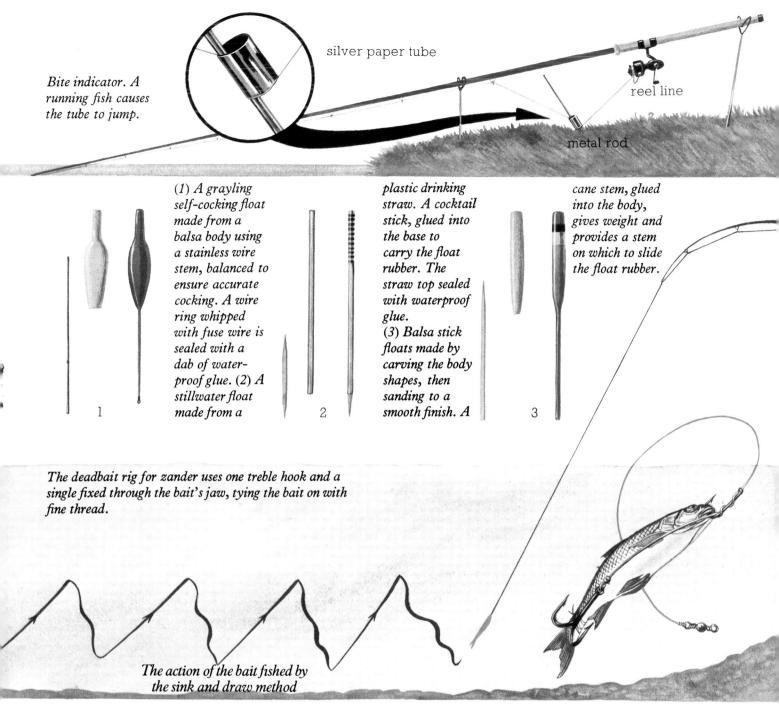

Bite indicator. A running fish causes the tube to jump.

silver paper tube

reel line

metal rod

(1) A grayling self-cocking float made from a balsa body using a stainless wire stem, balanced to ensure accurate cocking. A wire ring whipped with fuse wire is sealed with a dab of waterproof glue. (2) A stillwater float made from a

1

plastic drinking straw. A cocktail stick, glued into the base to carry the float rubber. The straw top sealed with waterproof glue.
(3) Balsa stick floats made by carving the body shapes, then sanding to a smooth finish. A

2

cane stem, glued into the body, gives weight and provides a stem on which to slide the float rubber.

3

The deadbait rig for zander uses one treble hook and a single fixed through the bait's jaw, tying the bait on with fine thread.

The action of the bait fished by the sink and draw method

take a fish bait in mid-water. A spinning rod will cope with the strength of all but the monster zander. Fish a deadbait rig, on which you can mount a small sprat, using the *sink and draw* technique. This is a fishing style that keeps you warm in the winter. You work your way along the river bank, making a couple of casts then moving on to search the next likely piece of river.

Cast the bait out and let it settle almost on the bottom. Give a couple of sharp turns to the reel handle which will make the bait rise in the water. Wait a while for the bait to flutter back to the river bed. Then draw the bait toward you with a slow, steady pull to the rod tip. Wind in line as you drop the rod tip. The action is repeated continually until the bait comes under the bank on which you are

standing. The zander sees a small fish that swims up, then falls back through the water. As he may think that it is wounded so he moves in to attack. I have found that a bite is shown by the line going solid. Then I have felt a few trembles, no doubt made as the zander turns the fish to take it into its mouth. That is when to strike hard. If you delay the strike, the fish may have swallowed the bait which will make a problem when unhooking the zander.

There is another fish that I like to go after in the wintertime—the grayling, which can be found in a number of trout streams. It is regarded as a coarse fish and will take a trotted worm. Ideally, you want a selfcocking float with very little lead so that the bait swims downstream in a natural way. Use the float rod and the lighter line for the maximum pleasure.

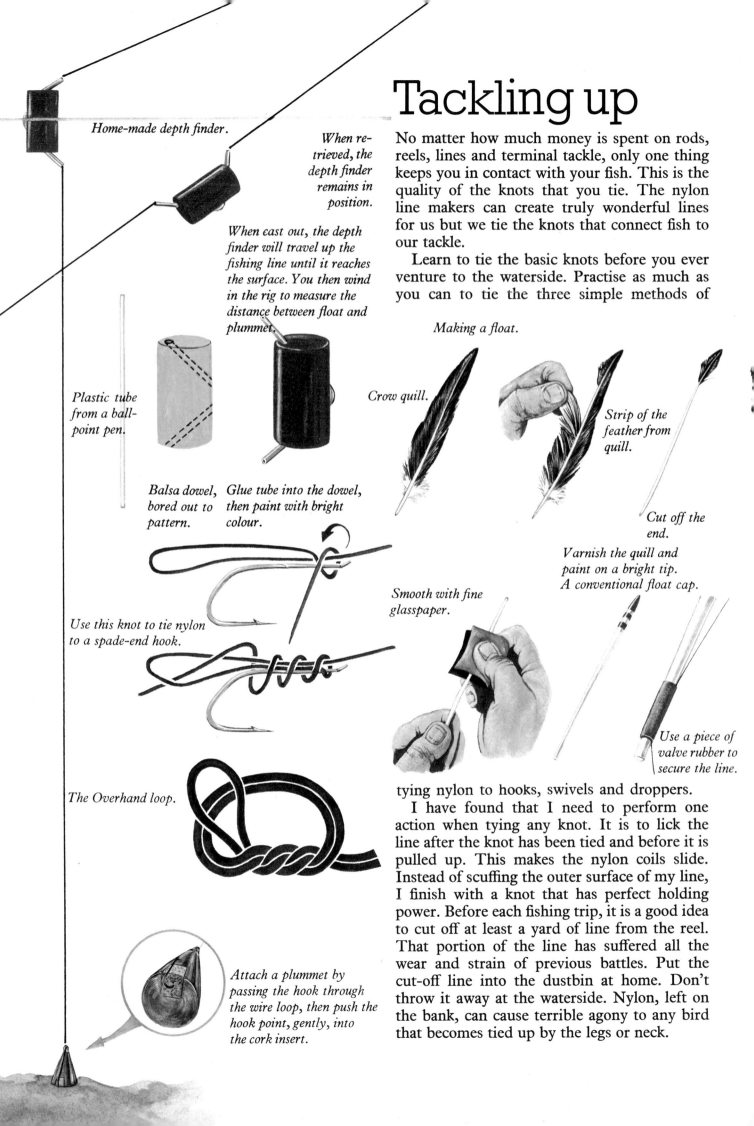

Home-made depth finder.

When retrieved, the depth finder remains in position.

When cast out, the depth finder will travel up the fishing line until it reaches the surface. You then wind in the rig to measure the distance between float and plummet.

Tackling up

No matter how much money is spent on rods, reels, lines and terminal tackle, only one thing keeps you in contact with your fish. This is the quality of the knots that you tie. The nylon line makers can create truly wonderful lines for us but we tie the knots that connect fish to our tackle.

Learn to tie the basic knots before you ever venture to the waterside. Practise as much as you can to tie the three simple methods of

Making a float.

Plastic tube from a ball-point pen.

Balsa dowel, bored out to pattern.

Glue tube into the dowel, then paint with bright colour.

Crow quill.

Strip of the feather from quill.

Cut off the end.

Varnish the quill and paint on a bright tip. A conventional float cap.

Smooth with fine glasspaper.

Use this knot to tie nylon to a spade-end hook.

Use a piece of valve rubber to secure the line.

The Overhand loop.

tying nylon to hooks, swivels and droppers.

I have found that I need to perform one action when tying any knot. It is to lick the line after the knot has been tied and before it is pulled up. This makes the nylon coils slide. Instead of scuffing the outer surface of my line, I finish with a knot that has perfect holding power. Before each fishing trip, it is a good idea to cut off at least a yard of line from the reel. That portion of the line has suffered all the wear and strain of previous battles. Put the cut-off line into the dustbin at home. Don't throw it away at the waterside. Nylon, left on the bank, can cause terrible agony to any bird that becomes tied up by the legs or neck.

Attach a plummet by passing the hook through the wire loop, then push the hook point, gently, into the cork insert.

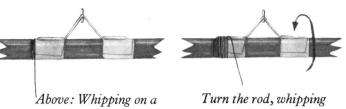

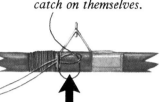

Above: Whipping on a rod ring—wrap several turns of thread so that they catch on themselves.

Turn the rod, whipping toward the ring.

Left: Place a loop of thread (arrowed) and continue to wrap the whipping. Cut off the thread, leaving a length of 3 inches. Pass it through the loop and then pull the loop of thread back under the whipping. This will trap the loose end.

Every tackle box should contain a disgorger. Even with instant reaction to a bite, there will always be the fish that is awkwardly hooked. The disgorger enables us to remove a hook painlessly. As you handle a fish, cup it under the belly, support the weight of the creature. Try not to grip it hard as this will cause it harm. A damp cloth comes in handy when you are holding a big fish. It stops you from removing the protective slime that covers the fish's scales.

Fishing is a sport that encourages a *do-it-yourself* attitude. There is so much satisfaction in catching a fish on something that you have made! Floats must be a perfect starting point. Stick floats, used to trot down the river, can be shaped from a balsa wood dowel with a penknife. The wood can be bought, for a few

Using a disgorger to remove the hook from the fish's jaw.

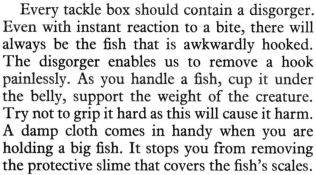

Hold your fish properly—cradle, rather than squeeze it.

Bank sticks have threaded ends to take keepnets and some patterns of rodrests.

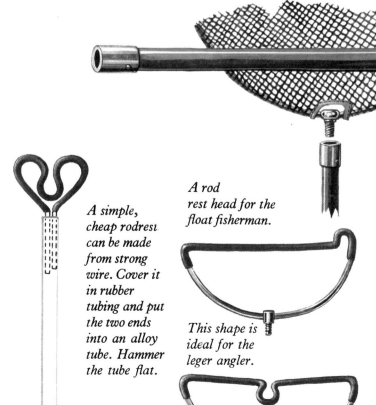

A simple, cheap rodrest can be made from strong wire. Cover it in rubber tubing and put the two ends into an alloy tube. Hammer the tube flat.

A rod rest head for the float fisherman.

This shape is ideal for the leger angler.

pence, from any model shop.

Keep a sharp eye open for large bird feathers that may be lying near to the waterside. Duck and crow feathers make ideal quill floats. Strip the fluff and flight feather from the quill. Then, lightly smooth the quill with fine glasspaper. A tiny slip of 15 amp fusewire is bent to form a ring for the line. Whip the metal tight with fine sewing thread, Terylene is best. A coat of varnish will seal the whipping and make the float watertight. You can paint a black ring around the top of the quill to make bite detection easier in choppy water.

45